100 Questions and Answers About Hispanics and Latinos

Michigan State University
School of Journalism

Read The Spirit Books

an imprint of
David Crumm Media, LLC
Canton, Michigan

For more information and further discussion, visit
news.jrn.msu.edu/culturalcompetence

Cover art and design by
Rick Nease
www.RickNeaseArt.com

Published by
Read The Spirit Books
an imprint of
David Crumm Media, LLC
42015 Ford Rd., Suite 234
Canton, Michigan, USA

For information about customized editions, bulk purchases
or permissions, contact David Crumm Media, LLC at info@
DavidCrummMedia.com

Contents

About the Series

The Michigan State University School of Journalism designed this series of guides as a journalistic tool to help replace bias and stereotypes with information. We create guides that are factual, clear and concise.

We begin these guides by asking people to tell us the questions they hear about themselves and others in their group in everyday, casual conversations with people who want to know about them. Some of the questions are simple. The answers almost never are, and one size does not fit all.

Sometimes, we must interpret the questions or look for the meaning behind them. We search for answers in studies, surveys and research. We ask experts. Our goal is to answer these first-level questions in ways that are accurate, authoritative and accessible. We respect the people who ask the questions and the people they address.

These guides are intended to be just the first step to more conversations and greater understanding.

Acknowledgments

Students who worked on this guide were members of the "Bias Busters" class in the Michigan State University School of Journalism. They are: Trisha Bellgowan, Jennifer Brown, Victoria Bujny, Julia Garvey, Alexandra Ilitch, Liz LeCrone, Hannah Middleton, Alice Naser, Casey O'Connell, Monica Reida, Simon Schuster, Chelsey Spinney, Hanna Sprague and Victoria Tomkinson. Matilyn Ozment helped on the project.

We are indebted to the people at the Pew Research Center's Hispanic Trends Project, http://www.pewhispanic.org/, and Director Mark Hugo Lopez, as well as the U.S. Census Bureau, the Gallup organization, the National Council of La Raza and others whose research is the background of this guide to cultural competence. Our most-cited resource is the Pew Research Center and its Hispanic Trends Project. It appears in the guide as Pew.

Experts in several areas patiently gave advice on the guide and we thank them for making it so much better. They include:

* Federico Subervi, professor, Kent State University School of Journalism & Mass Communication

* Maggie Rivas-Rodriguez, associate professor, University of Texas at Austin
* Mia Moody-Ramirez, associate professor, Baylor University
* Teresa Puente, associate professor of journalism, Columbia College Chicago
* Cindy E. Rodríguez, journalist-in-residence, Emerson College
* Diana Rios, associate professor of communication sciences, University of Connecticut
* Kevin Olivas, recruitment and guidance manager, National Association of Hispanic Journalists
* Bruno Takahashi, assistant professor, Michigan State University School of Journalism
* Sheila M. Contreras, director, Michigan State University Chicano/Latino Studies Program
* Diana Rivera, Chicana/o Latina/o studies bibliographer, Michigan State University Libraries
* Ignacio Andrade, Office for Inclusion and Intercultural Initiatives, Michigan State University
* Susan E. Reed, supervising attorney, Michigan Immigrant Rights Center
* Al Flores, director of community relations, Michigan Department of Civil Rights
* John Golaszewski, director of business & community affairs, Michigan Department of Civil Rights

Thank you,

Dr. Manuel Chavez, project editor
Joe Grimm, series editor

Michigan State University School of Journalism
College of Communication Arts and Sciences

Introduction

By Manuel Chavez

This brief, 100-answer look at the 53 million Americans called Hispanics or Latinos covers origins, identity, citizenship, education, occupation, health, culture, income, origin and more.

Hispanics or Latinos? Both can be correct. It all depends on how individuals identify themselves and it could be because of origin, language or tradition. A Hispanic could be of Mexican, Puerto Rican or Cuban origin, and a Latino could be, too. In many cases, a second- or third-generation Hispanic/Latino born in the United States might not even speak Spanish and yet identify as one or the other.

The United States is often portrayed as a nation of immigrants, but as history shows, Native Americans and many Hispanics were in the land before Europeans arrived. The United States-Mexico War caused many Mexicans and Spanish-Mexicans in what is now the Southwest to wake up with a new citizenship after the peace treaty of 1848. Without moving, many acquired a new government, language and citizenship. They did not cross over the border; the border crossed over them. Migration did not start as an important process between the two countries until the Mexican Revolution of 1910-1921.

Similarly, after the Spanish-American War ended in 1898, Puerto Ricans found that their original colonizer, Spain, had ceded the island to the United States. In 1917, Congress granted Puerto Ricans U.S. citizenship.

Migration followed, but for different reasons: political turmoil in the case of Mexico and economic pressures in Puerto Rico. Yet both migrations started a diaspora of Hispanics to the United States. Cuba followed, primarily because of politics. Other pressures pushed more waves of immigration.

Composition

Hispanics make up almost one-fifth of the total U.S. population, 17 percent, up from 13 percent in 2000. Projections show that by 2050, Hispanics will account for nearly one-third of the U.S. population.

This guide explains how two-thirds of Hispanics are concentrated in five states. However, five other states have seen the fastest growth of Hispanic population since 2000. Census data show Alabama with 158 percent population growth, South Carolina and Tennessee with 154 percent growth, Kentucky with 132 percent and South Dakota with 129 percent.

Almost two thirds of Hispanics in the United States are Mexican. There's a significant gap before the second largest group. Puerto Ricans are 9 percent of the Hispanic population, followed by Salvadorans and Cubans at 4 percent each and Dominicans at 3 percent.

Contrary to common belief, the increasing number of Hispanics is due to births and fertility, not immigration. From 2000 to 2010, the Hispanic population grew by 7.2 million due to births and 4.2 million due to immigration. Previously, immigration had matched or exceeded growth due to births.

The fertility rate of Hispanic women is 2.4 births per woman, higher than for all minority groups, and 25 percent higher than the rate for white women of 1.8.

Birth rates have implications in U.S. education from K-12 classrooms to colleges. According to Pew, Hispanics now make up one-fourth of all students in public schools. Hispanic college enrollment increased by 265,000, and Hispanics now make up 16.5 percent of all college students. The Hispanic high school dropout rate is declining, too.

Politics

As diverse as Hispanics are, their politics are also divergent. Generally, pundits say that Hispanics tend to be more liberal, but in reality they are as split as the rest of America. Latinos are liberal, conservative and independent. They are Democrats and Republicans, they belong to the tea party movement, the Green Party and the Libertarian Party.

Although their representation in political office does not equal their proportion in the population, it is growing. Some of the most prominent Hispanics serving in both the Clinton and Bush administrations were of Mexican, Puerto Rican and Cuban origin. President Barack Obama appointed Sonia Sotomayor of Puerto Rican origin to the U.S. Supreme Court.

The assumption that Hispanics lean Democratic because they are laborers, migrants, hourly or unionized workers is not accurate. Hispanics have one of the highest rates of entrepreneurship and small-business ownership in the United States and these Hispanics tend to identify with the Republican Party. Hispanic political affiliation mirrors the larger U.S. electorate.

The so-called Hispanic Agenda in national politics is as diverse as the American Agenda. Hispanics are portrayed as having three interests: immigration, border control and social welfare. However, the Hispanic political agenda is determined more by generations. While recent migrants and first generations may identify those issues as important, subsequent generations focus on education, jobs and health. The agenda is not homogenized. On the contrary, the agenda is as diverse as Hispanics themselves. Generation, income, occupation and education are more likely to determine the areas that Hispanics pursue politically—in any political party.

The power of Hispanics in national politics is growing. Hispanics had an impact in 2012 swing states and it is clear that to win the presidency, candidates need the Hispanic vote.

Health

Hispanic health is affected by language or culture, access to proper care and insurance. According to the Centers for Disease Control and Prevention, leading heath issues among the Hispanic population are heart disease, cancer, diabetes, asthma, COPD and obesity. The rate of obesity is higher for Hispanics than non-Hispanics and in 2010 Mexican-American children between 6 and 17 were 60 percent more likely than non-Hispanic white children to be overweight, according to the Office of Minority Health. In 2011, 78 percent of Mexican-American women in the U.S. were obese, compared to 60.3 percent of white women. Still, according to the Population Reference Bureau, the life expectancy of Hispanics in 2010 was 81.2 years compared to 78.8 for the non-Hispanic white population. This is the "Hispanic Paradox" of living longer, despite having more health problems. The reason is thought to be stronger social networks and community support. Another explanation may be less tobacco use within the Hispanic population. Although Hispanics live longer, they are more likely to spend more years disabled compared to whites, according to the Population Reference Bureau.

Immigration

Immigration unifies and separates Hispanics. Some support relaxed legislation that allows more open-door policies and facilitates family reunification. Others want more controls and limits. How is it possible that immigration can be a

Where do Hispanics and Latinos in the U.S. come from?

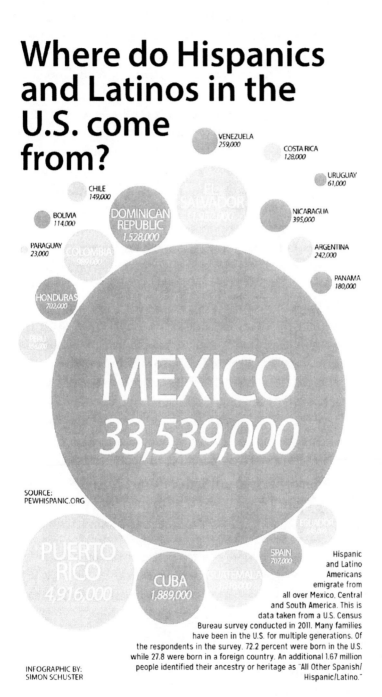

VENEZUELA
259,000

COSTA RICA
128,000

URUGUAY
61,000

CHILE
149,000

BOLIVIA
114,000

DOMINICAN REPUBLIC
1,528,000

EL SALVADOR
1,648,000

NICARAGUA
395,000

PARAGUAY
23,000

COLOMBIA
989,000

ARGENTINA
242,000

PANAMA
180,000

HONDURAS
702,000

PERU
556,000

MEXICO
33,539,000

SOURCE:
PEWHISPANIC.ORG

ECUADOR
645,000

PUERTO RICO
4,916,000

CUBA
1,889,000

GUATEMALA
1,216,000

SPAIN
707,000

Hispanic and Latino Americans emigrate from all over Mexico, Central and South America. This is data taken from a U.S. Census Bureau survey conducted in 2011. Many families have been in the U.S. for multiple generations. Of the respondents in the survey, 72.2 percent were born in the U.S. while 27.8 were born in a foreign country. An additional 1.67 million people identified their ancestry or heritage as "All Other Spanish/Hispanic/Latino."

INFOGRAPHIC BY:
SIMON SCHUSTER

polarizing factor among Hispanics? Simple. It is a generational issue. Recent immigrants and the first generation born in the United States tend to be more supportive of lax policies on immigration. Subsequent generations are more inclined to support more restriction.

This guide deals with waves of immigration, whether pulled by the U.S. need for workers or pushed by economic need and politics. All created pressure for families to reunite.

Many were motivated by economics, others by politics and others simply to reunite their families. Likewise, there are variations in the makeup of each wave based on age, gender, education and English proficiency.

The notion that most Hispanics have arrived in the United States as undocumented, illegally or as visa abusers is not entirely accurate. Many Hispanics live in the United States with proper documentation. This includes people with temporary permits, permanent resident visas, family reunification allowances, company transfers, tourist, investor and student visas. In many states, corporations with operations in Mexico have a significant movement of staff in both directions. These individuals tend to be professionals in engineering, business, logistics, research and development.

Undocumented or illegal immigration has happened not only across the border with Mexico, but also across the border with Canada and through coastal ports more accessible to Europe and Asia. Many of these immigrants arrive with tourist permits to later engage in work, which is strictly prohibited. The most widely known group, however, are individuals who enter from Mexico and who spread to different states, from California to South Carolina and as far as New York. Recently, they are more likely to be Central Americans from Guatemala, El Salvador, Honduras and Nicaragua. Mexicans are not crossing the border as they used to, in part because of a strengthening Mexican economy.

Family reunification is one of the most difficult stories of immigration. This is when adolescents and children cross into the United States to join parents or family. In some cases a parent accompanies them, but in many cases, they are alone. The deportation process for minors is complicated, since in many cases information about reaching their family members is inaccurate or incomplete.

Destination is another facet. While Hispanics are concentrated in the Southwest and Florida, in the past 10 years there has been a trend for migrants to move to states that have not historically had a large Hispanic presence.

Regardless of legal status, recent immigrants are less likely to move back to their countries of origin. There is a trend toward permanent settlement. This is due to the difficulty in crossing the border, where they face new technologies and more border patrol officers. For many, it is virtually impossible to go back and forth. Many migrants stay in the United States for up to five years, save their income, and then return home to invest in a small business to build their family houses.

Finally, new immigrants are arriving with more education. Traditionally, the educational level of undocumented immigrants was low, but recent immigrants are more likely to have more than a high school education, including professional and English skills and even a college education. For this group, it is relatively easier to get a job.

Culture

Hispanic culture is rich, diverse and dynamic. Food and drink, traditions and music have historically transitioned to the mainstream American fabric. This is a remarkable achievement not often seen in a culture as ethnocentric as America's.

Hispanic architecture, for instance, has heavily influenced the look of California, Arizona, Texas and Florida. It has extended to many suburbs. Styles reminiscent of old Spanish-Mexican patios, hacienda roofs and tiles, open kitchens, fountains, gardens and plants are popular all over the country. Ironically, in many areas where there has been a persistent backlash against Latinos, as in Arizona, the most popular architectural style happens to be of Mexican origin.

Food and drink is another manifestation of Hispanic culture. Foods ranging from the Mexican mole, tacos, burritos and enchiladas to Cuban masitas de puerco, ropa vieja, to Argentinian churrascos, to Peruvian ceviche, and to empanadas of anything have caught on in the United States. Salsas with multiple flavors and spice intensities rival ketchup at the condiment counter. Tortillas are selling more than white bread, and tamales and burritos are a popular choice for quick lunches in major metro areas across the nation. Food trucks of Hispanic food that started as taco trucks in downtown Los Angeles have popped up all over the country. Corporate franchises of Hispanic foods attract investment. Margaritas, tequila, Mexican beer, mojito and pisco have replaced other spirits and drinks in popularity. And the popularity of churros as a sweet dessert is big at many major sports events and state fairs.

This guide explains how Hispanic holidays and celebrations have taken root in U.S. culture. Piñatas that were once very hard to find are sold in almost any children's or party store. They have become a standby in American family celebrations.

Hispanic music has also gone mainstream. Salsa and other forms of Caribbean dances are popular among young and old dancers. Artists such as Carlos Santana, Gloria Estefan, Jennifer Lopez, Los Lobos and Linda Ronstadt doubled their potential audience by singing in Spanish and English.

We hope the answers to these 100 simple questions, the kind we hear at work and at lunch counters, will lead you to a deeper understanding of this growing part of U.S. life.

Identity

1 Why does the title of this guide refer to Hispanics and Latinos? How are the terms different?

Hispanic means "of Spain or Spanish-speaking countries." Latino means from or related to Latin America. Some Spanish-speaking countries, such as Spain, are not in Latin America. Some Latin American countries, such as Brazil, are not Spanish-speaking countries. It can be confusing. Latin also refers to languages that developed out of ancient Rome, including French and Italian. But Latino as used in the United States refers to the geography of Latin America, not necessarily to languages.

2 How did these words become official terms?

The U.S. Census Bureau used the term "Hispanic" in a question in its 1970 long form, but not in the entire census. The 1980 census included the term. Many people objected to "Hispanic," calling it an inadequate, non-Spanish word imposed by the government that rang of colonization. Some preferred the word "Latino." The federal Office of Management and Budget made the standards change in 1997 and "Latino" was added to the 2000 census form. Today, the Census Bureau uses both terms.

3 Are there U.S. regional or state preferences for these terms?

The Pew Research Center's Hispanic Trends Project found that roughly half of the Hispanic and Latino people in the United States have no strong preference for either term. There is one big exception, however. In Texas, 46 percent said in 2013 that they preferred to be called Hispanic while only 8 percent preferred Latino. No other state comes close to that. This guide uses the terms interchangeably.

4 So people can be one and not the other?

Yes. Individuals decide how to identify themselves. A 2013 report by the Pew Hispanic Trends Project showed that 54 percent of the people in this group said they describe themselves with their ancestors' origin, such as Mexican, Puerto Rican or Salvadoran. Twenty-three percent call themselves American. Twenty percent use Hispanic or Latino or Latina. Other terms include "Chicano," "Tejano" or "Boricua." We'll explore these one at a time.

5 What does "Latina" mean?

Spanish grammar uses gender, so there are masculine and feminine nouns. "Latina" is the feminine form of "Latino" and means a woman or girl.

6 What do "Chicano" and "Chicana" mean?

Historically, these terms have been chosen by people of Mexican descent who identify with the 1960s U.S. civil rights movement and the struggle of migrant agricultural workers. The terms was originally considered derogatory. However, the Chicano movement during the 1960s adopted these names in response to discrimination against Mexican Americans working under unfair labor and social conditions. These terms announce pride in indigenous ancestry, which was a significant ideological element of the Chicano movement.

7 What about Chican@?

This post-Internet construction simplifies "Chicano/ Chicana" or "Chicano and/or Chicana." Some academic studies departments have put this in their names. According to the University of Wisconsin at Madison, "The @ ending ('a' at the center of 'o') offers a simultaneous presentation of both the feminine and masculine word endings of Chicana, Chicano, Latina, and Latino and allows the reader/speaker to choose the form she or he prefers."

8 What about Tejano?

Tejano means a Texan of Mexican descent. Tejano derives from "Coahuiltejano," a name given to the citizens of the Mexican State of Coahuila y Tejas, now Texas. Tejano culture includes folk music synthesized from European and Mexican styles and contributions to Tex-Mex cuisine. Hispanic and Anglo-Saxon settlers who lived in the area during the 18th century created a bilingualism that later shaped the Tejano language.

9 And what is Boricua?

Puerto Rico was formerly known as Borikén, a self-governed island inhabited by the Taino people. The arrival of Spanish settlers during the 16th century decimated the Taino population and many were forced into assimilation. The term Boricua is a derivative of Borikén and connotes pride in Puerto Rican origins.

10 What race are Latinos and Hispanics?

According to the U.S. Census Bureau, this is not a race, but an ethnicity. This means shared language and cultural traditions. Hispanics and Latinos can be of any race and have a wide range of physical characteristics, including dark to light skin and hair. People of every race live in Latin American and Spanish-speaking countries. Like other Americans, many people identify with both a nationality or ethnicity and they can be of any race.

Demographics

Hispanics and Latinos in the U.S.

Places of origin

Spanish speaking

Non-Spanish speaking

illustration by Cody T. Harrell

11 How many Hispanic people live in the United States?

According to the U.S. Census Bureau, there were 53 million Hispanics in the United States on July 1, 2012, making it the nation's largest minority group. They represent about 17 percent of the U.S. population. The Census Bureau projects there will be 128.8 million Hispanics by mid-century, and that they will comprise 31 percent of the nation's population.

12 What are their places of origin?

Almost two-thirds, 65 percent, have Mexican ancestry, according to the U.S. Census Bureau. The second largest place of origin, Puerto Rico, has almost 5 million people in the United Stated and the District of Columbia and 3.6 million in Puerto Rico. The next three nationalities, each between 3 and 4 percent, are Salvadoran, Cuban and Dominican. The rest have ancestries throughout South and Central America and parts of the Caribbean.

13 Which states have the largest Hispanic populations?

Almost half of Hispanics live in California and Texas. California has the largest numbers of Hispanics in the nation, about 14.4 million, or 38 percent of the state's population, and is now the largest single ethnic group in California. Texas is second in total number with 10 million, or 19 percent. Florida, with 4.5 million, is 8 percent Hispanic. New Mexico, with almost a million, is the state with the highest concentration of Hispanics at 47 percent of the state's population. By contrast, in some states, such as West Virginia, Maine and Vermont, Hispanics are only 1 percent of the population.

14 Do Hispanics in the United States live in cities or rural areas?

According to the U.S. Census Bureau's American Community Survey data, almost half of the nation's Hispanics live in 10 major metropolitan areas with populations of more than 1 million. The Hispanic population is highly concentrated in urban areas. Just 100 counties are home to 71 percent of the Hispanic population. Nine percent of all Hispanics in the United States live in Los Angeles County.

15 Didn't part of the United States used to be part of Mexico?

Yes. At the end of the Mexican-American War in 1848, Mexico was forced to give up about half of its territory in the treaty of Guadalupe Hidalgo. This included all of the present-day states of California, Nevada, Utah and Texas and portions of what became New Mexico, Arizona, Colorado and Wyoming. In 1853, land was purchased from Mexico to extend the southern portions of present-day Arizona and New Mexico through the Gadsden Purchase.

16 Is Puerto Rico a country, colony or commonwealth?

This is complicated. Spain held Puerto Rico as a colony for more than 400 years and ceded it to the United States in 1898 at the end of the Spanish-American War. It has been under U.S. rule as an unincorporated territory ever since, but is not a state. Puerto Ricans were made citizens in 1917, though they had not requested it. In 1952, with Congressional approval, Puerto Ricans voted to become a commonwealth. This did not fundamentally change the relationship between Puerto Rico and the United States.

17 Why is Puerto Rico a territory and not a state or a country?

This is a continuing issue in Puerto Rico. Puerto Rico has voted on its status in 1967, 1993 and 1998, but results did not overwhelmingly support one status over another. A non-binding vote in 2012 had a ballot with two parts. The first part asked whether people were satisfied with the current arrangement. Fifty-three percent voted no. On the second part of the ballot, three options were presented. Statehood received the most votes, but half a million voters chose none of the three options. No-option votes, combined with votes for independence, meant more than 55 percent of the voters did not choose statehood.

18 Do people living in Puerto Rico vote in U.S. elections?

Despite the fact that Puerto Ricans are U.S. citizens, Puerto Ricans living on the island are not allowed to vote in national elections. Only residents of states are authorized by the Constitution to do so. Puerto Ricans who live in the United States can vote for any position on the ballot, including president. Puerto Rico does not have representation in Congress.

19 Do Puerto Ricans in Puerto Rico pay U.S. taxes?

Those living in Puerto Rico pay Social Security and Medicare payroll taxes to the U.S. government and are eligible for some, but not all, benefits. They pay their income taxes to the government of Puerto Rico, but not to the U.S. federal government.

20 What is Hispaniola?

This is the large Caribbean Island where Christopher Columbus made his first settlement. The name means "Isle of Spain." It contains two countries: The Dominican Republic on the east, where Columbus landed, and Haiti on the west.

21 Are the countries in Hispaniola Hispanic, then?

Spanish is the official language of The Dominican Republic, but Haiti was colonized by the French, and people who had lived under slavery later made it independent. Haiti's main languages are French and Haitian Creole. Although its Caribbean neighbors are Spanish-speaking countries and they share some concerns, Haiti's residents are not Hispanic.

Language

22 What languages do Hispanics speak in the United States?

This varies. One important factor is how long they or their families have been in the United States. According to Pew research from 2011, 38 percent of immigrant Hispanics said they speak English very well and 91 percent said they speak Spanish very well. However, among Hispanics whose families have been in the United States for two or more generations, the numbers were almost reversed. Ninety-six percent said they could speak English very well and 47 said they speak Spanish very well. One should not assume that a Hispanic person must speak Spanish or meet certain cultural conditions to be authentic or valid. Another factor is country of origin. Remember that although a high percentage of Latinos come from Spanish-speaking countries, some do not. Brazil, for example, is a Portuguese-speaking country. And some know indigenous languages in addition to English and Spanish.

23 How prevalent is bilingualism?

This also varies. According to a 2012 Pew report, 38 percent of Hispanic adults said they were proficient in both English and Spanish. Thirty-eight percent said they were Spanish dominant and 24 percent were English dominant. This shifted with the generations. Thirty-three percent of immigrants reported they were bilingual and 61 percent said they were Spanish dominant. In the second generation, 53 percent were bilingual. By the third generation, 29 percent said they were bilingual and 69 percent said they were English dominant.

24 What is Spanglish?

Spanglish is an informal hybrid of Spanish and English. It is used among people who know both languages and who switch between languages when one language describes what they are trying to say better than the other. Linguists call that code switching. In 2009, 23 percent of Hispanics between 16 and 25 told Pew researchers they used Spanglish most of the time and another 47 percent said they used it sometimes.

25 Are there different dialects of Spanish?

Spanish has many regional dialects. Generally, Spanish speakers understand one another because they are speaking the same language. It can be difficult at times when dialects are extremely different and there can be differences in idioms. It is similar to different dialects of English in the United States, Australia or Great Britain. Despite differences, language joins culture as a powerful unifying force. Contrast that with Asia, where there are large language barriers among countries.

26 Do accents tell us where people are from?

Accents do not pinpoint where people are from. Accents develop from how, where and when languages are learned. Moving to a new place and mixing with new people can change an accent. If you are curious about someone's origin, it is better to ask or wait for him or her to bring it up.

27 What is the letter ñ?

In the Spanish alphabet, this is an additional letter, not just an n with an accent mark, which is called a tilde. It is called an eñe and is pronounced "enye." It is used in many words. Substituting a plain n, a whole different letter, can change the word. In speech, this letter sounds like the middle sound in canyon. In fact, the Spanish word for canyon is cañón.

28 Spanish can sound fast to me. Is it spoken quickly?

Researchers at the Université de Lyon recorded speakers of seven different languages to see whether there is actually a difference in how much information syllables carry and how quickly they are spoken. They found that some languages use more syllables than some others to say the same thing but that speakers complete the phrase in the same time. For example, in English we say, "the green car," which has three syllables. In Spanish, that is "el coche es verde," which has six syllables.

29 What is the English-only movement?

This is an effort to make English the official language of the United States. About half the states have adopted English-only laws. Opponents say such laws are unnecessary, divisive and even racist.

Religion

30 Are Hispanics more religious than other Americans?

According to Pew research in 2011, 83 percent of Hispanics identified with a specific religion, compared to 80 percent for all Americans. Hispanics were also more likely than Americans in general to engage in daily prayer or regularly attend services.

31 Are U.S. Hispanics mostly Catholic?

Yes, they are, though the proportion who call themselves Protestant is rising. A Pew study in 2012 found that 58 percent said they were Catholic in 2012. That was down from 62 percent in 2011 and 67 percent in 2010. By comparison, 23 percent of all Americans say they are Catholic.

32 How are Hispanics changing the U.S. Catholic Church?

Younger Hispanics are more likely than other Catholics to choose charismatic Catholic churches. Some are leaving for Protestant churches and they are more likely than other Protestants to choose "born again" evangelical churches. A 2011 Pew study found that 19 percent of Hispanics were Protestants, compared to half of the U.S. general public.

33 Is Pope Francis the first Latin American pope?

Yes. Pope Francis is the son of Italian immigrants to Argentina. Latinos in the United States acknowledge that he is by birth Latin American, but do not necessarily consider him "Latino."

34 Who is Our Lady of Guadalupe?

She is the symbol of the Catholic faith in Mexico and among Mexicans and considered the patron saint of the Americas by the Catholic Church. She appeared in 1531 to an Indian convert to Christianity, Juan Diego, at the site of a shrine to an Aztec goddess. Several places in Latin America have local manifestations of the Virgin Mary as patroness. They include Our Lady of Charity in Cuba; Our Lady of Peace in El Salvador; and Our Lady of Chiquinquirá, in Colombia, among others.

Social Norms

35 Do Latinos generally follow a low or high physical-contact culture?

People in different countries have been observed and categorized according to the degree of physical contact. North America, northern Europe and Asia have been classified as low-contact. People in Latin America, southern and eastern Europe and the Middle East are generally more high-contact.

36 What are preferences for personal space?

Latino personal space preferences tend to be closer than for most other Americans. Latinos may view a person who stands several feet away as being distant.

37 Are Latinos generally more emotional or expressive than other Americans?

Of course, emotionalism and expressiveness are not the same thing and individual behaviors vary. In 2012, Gallup asked people in 150 countries whether they had felt five positive and five negative emotions in the previous day. From their answers, Gallup ranked countries on how emotional its people are. Gallup ranked people in the Philippines as most emotional and people in Singapore as least emotional. The top 10 most emotional countries included El Salvador, Colombia and then a tie among 11 countries for sixth place. They included Chile, Costa Rica, Guatemala, Bolivia, Ecuador, the Dominican Republic, Peru, Nicaragua and the United States. Mexico was rated as less emotional than the United States.

38 Are Latinos traditionally modest about their accomplishments?

Cultures range from individualistic to collectivistic. Individualistic cultures are oriented around the achievements of the person. Collectivistic cultures focus on groups such as family, community and country. The United States places higher value on individual accomplishments. Hispanic culture is more collective and emphasizes group success.

Politics

39 How do Hispanics align politically?

According to a Gallup survey of voters in 2012, 51 percent of Hispanics identified with or leaned Democratic while 24 percent said they identified with or leaned Republican. Democrats have carried the Hispanic vote in every presidential election since 1980. One of the largest spreads occurred in 2012 when Democratic President Barack Obama won 71 percent of the Hispanic vote and Republican candidate Mitt Romney won 27 percent. Still, a 2011 Pew study showed that Hispanics are almost as likely as the U.S. population at large to identify themselves as socially conservative. One should not assume political affiliation on the basis of ethnicity.

40 What are top political concerns for Hispanics today?

Although this varies among immigrants and U.S.-born people, according to a 2012 USA Today/ Gallup Poll, Hispanics prioritized immigration, health care and unemployment. Hispanics were also concerned with economic growth, the gap between rich and poor, education and the federal budget deficit. The poll showed that economic issues, specifically unemployment and growth, generally matter more than immigration to Hispanic voters.

41 How much weight does the Hispanic vote carry in U.S elections?

Analysts said that the Hispanic vote made a notable difference in the 2012 presidential election and helped President Barack Obama win re-election. Without their votes, the outcome of the election could have been different. The Hispanic vote was also influential in swing states such as Colorado, Florida and Nevada. As a large and growing part of the population, Hispanic political influence is growing.

42 What is turnout like among Hispanics voters?

The Census Bureau reported that more than 11 million Hispanics voted in the 2012 presidential election, making up almost 8.5 percent of the vote. Only 48 percent of eligible Hispanics voted, however. According to the Bipartisan Policy Center, voter turnout for the general population in presidential elections has been around 60 percent. Unexercised Hispanic voting power has been called "the sleeping giant." The National Council of La Raza began a campaign in 2014 to register a quarter million Hispanic voters by the November elections.

43 Are Hispanics represented proportionately in government?

They are not represented according to their proportion in the population, but representation is growing. Thirty-one Hispanics, including three senators, were elected to Congress in 2012. The National Association of Latino Elected and Appointed Officials represents 6,000 officials at all levels of government. There have been more than 60 Hispanic members of Congress and nine U.S. senators. The first Hispanic U.S. senator took office in 1928. The first Hispanic congressman joined Congress in 1877.

44 Who are some nationally prominent Hispanic politicians?

In recent times, Sonia Sotomayor became an associate justice of the U.S. Supreme Court. She was born in the Bronx, N.Y., to Puerto Rican parents. Marco Rubio, R-Fla.; Ted Cruz, R-Texas; and Bob Menendez, D-N.J., serve in the U.S. Senate. Rubio was born in Florida to Cuban parents. Cruz was born in Canada to a Cuban father and an Italian and Irish mother. Menendez was born in New York City to Cuban parents. Former Los Angeles Mayor Antonio Villagrasia, who was term limited in 2013, is Mexican American. Bill Richardson, whose parents are of Mexican descent, has been governor of New Mexico, a UN ambassador, energy secretary and a U.S. congressman. The Castro brothers, Chicanos from San Antonio, include U.S. Rep. Joaquin, D-Texas, and twin brother Julián, mayor of San Antonio.

Immigration

45 What draws Latinos to the United States?

A Pew study in 2011 found these reasons:

- 55 percent: economic opportunity
- 24 percent: family reasons
- 9 percent: educational opportunities
- 5 percent: conflict or persecution in home country
- 7 percent: other

46 What are the "waves" of Latino immigration to the United States?

1. The first wave was during the California Gold Rush, just after the Mexican-American War (1846-1848). The Treaty of Guadalupe Hidalgo called for Mexico to cede much of its land to the United States and offered naturalization to about 100,000 people who had been Mexican citizens.

2. The second wave occurred between 1930 until after World War II. Puerto Ricans who were facing unemployment and underemployment came to the United States seeking work. Throughout the 1960s and 1970s, there was a mass migration of Cubans to the United States.

3. Another wave occurred during World War II in 1941, as American farms hired Mexican labor.

4. In the 1970s and 1980s, the United States experienced a wave of immigrants from Latin American countries such as El Salvador, Guatemala, Honduras and Nicaragua due to people trying to escape political turbulence and violence.

5. The most recent wave occurred from about 2000 onward. Latinos have been migrating to the United States seeking economic opportunities and escaping violence. Specifically, there has been an influx of people from Mexico, Argentina, Chile, Columbia, Peru and Ecuador.

47 Why do some Latinos stay in the United States without documentation?

For some of the same reasons as people of other countries: for better opportunities. Emily Ryo, a law professor at the University of Southern California, is author of the 2013 study, "Why People Take the Risk of Illegal Immigration." She wrote that the wish for economic opportunity or to be with family is just part of the picture. Also, "perceptions about the legitimacy of U.S. legal authority, the morality of violating U.S. immigration laws, and social norms on illegal border crossings are significantly related to people's intentions to migrate illegally."

48 Are most Latinos in the United States today immigrants?

No. According to a U.S. Census Bureau report in 2011, 63.8 percent of the country's Latino population is U.S.-born. Among Latino origin groups, Mexicans have the highest share born in the U.S. at 65 percent. The proportions are lower among other groups. Thirty-six percent of Guatemalans, 42 percent of Cubans and 44 percent of Dominicans are U.S. born.

49 Do most Latino immigrants come to the United States legally?

Since the 1990s, undocumented immigration has outpaced legal immigration. There can be no accurate count of the number as individuals wish to avoid detection. The federal Department of Homeland Security and the Pew Research Center estimates are considered the best and say there are 10 million to 12 million undocumented immigrants in the United States. It's important to note that not all undocumented immigrants are Latino. According to Pew Research, about 75 percent of all undocumented immigrants are from Latin America.

50 Does the Latino community support U.S. immigration policies?

This is influenced by the length of time an individual's family has been in the country and the person's citizenship. Fifty-nine percent of Latinos surveyed by Pew in 2011 indicated that they disapproved of the way the Obama administration had handled deportations. Twenty-six percent said they personally knew someone who had been deported or detained by immigration officials in the previous 12 months.

51 What is the "DREAM Act?"

The DREAM Act stands for Development, Relief and Education for Alien Minors. It is a proposal first introduced in the U.S. Senate in 2001 to provide legal residency to undocumented youth who meet several criteria. Those include arrival in the United States as a minor, completing a high school diploma and completing two years in the military or at a four-year institution of higher learning. Supporters say the DREAM Act would help people and benefit the country economically. Opponents say it rewards people for breaking the law and encourages illegal immigration.

52 What is DACA?

DACA stands for Deferred Action for Childhood Arrivals. This program provides temporary relief from deportation and employment authorization for individuals who would be eligible for the DREAM Act were it to become law. DACA was created under the president's executive authority to grant certain classes of people "deferred action" on their immigration cases. It was announced by Obama in June of 2012 and can be renewed. It could be terminated at any time by executive action. To date, more than 550,000 young undocumented immigrants have applied for deferred action.

53 What are the top immigration policy concerns for Latinos?

The legalization component of proposed immigration reform has focused on pathways to citizenship, but Latinos and Asian Americans say they have a different priority. They told Pew researchers that they are more interested in seeing an end to the threat of deportation.

54 Is U.S. immigration more difficult for Latinos?

It can be. Several aspects of immigration law were designed to punish and exclude Latinos as part of an anti-Latino immigration backlash. The law focuses several punitive measures on people who entered without inspection rather than on those who have stayed beyond the length of their visas. Non-inspected entry happens most frequently on the Southwest border. So, though the law is neutral on its face, it excludes a disproportionate number of Latino immigrants from options that exist to legalize one's immigration status through family or employment relationships. Social and family networks might ease the process.

55 What is the "Drop the I-Word" campaign?

Started in 2010 by the Applied Race Center, now Race Forward, it objects to the labeling of immigrants who do not have documentation as "illegal." In 2013, the Associated Press changed its stylebook, which is used by hundreds of news outlets, to drop the term. The AP's reasoning went like this: "The Stylebook no longer sanctions the term 'illegal immigrant' or the use of 'illegal' to describe a person. Instead, it tells users that 'illegal' should describe only an action, such as immigrating or staying illegally." Other alternatives are undocumented immigrant or unauthorized immigrant.

56 What is a green card?

A green card is a United States Permanent Resident Card. It is actually a pink identification card that allows an immigrant to reside and live permanently in the United States. Green-card holders are also able to work in the U.S., to travel and to receive some government benefits. A green-card holder is not a U.S. citizen but can live in the United States permanently. It can be insulting to ask Latinos born in the United States and Puerto Ricans whether they have a green card, as they are U.S. citizens by birth.

57 What are the differences between permanent residency and citizenship?

When U.S. Citizenship and Immigration Services grants permanent residency, people have the right to legally work and live in the United States. In general, one must become a permanent legal resident before applying for citizenship. Citizens have more rights than permanent residents. These rights include: voting in U.S. elections, traveling on a U.S. passport, working as a federal employee, citizenship for one's minor children who are also permanent residents, and more federal benefits.

58 What are remittances?

Remittance is the term used when people send money from one country to people in another. Money is usually sent through electronic fund transfers. Remittances are a key source of support in many families and communities. Pew reported that in 2013 migrants, who send most of the money, transferred $22 billion in remittances to Mexico and $31.8 billion to all other Spanish-speaking Latin American nations.

59 Are Latinos profiled at borders?

Yes, though the U.S. Supreme Court has held that immigration agents working near the border with Mexico may not use apparent ancestry as the sole basis for detaining a person. Latinos are profiled at other U.S. borders, too.

60 Are they profiled at airports?

Yes, Latinos are profiled at airports, too. There have been complaints about profiling of Latinos at several airports. More than 30 Transportation Safety Administration officials told The New York Times that a program to spot potential terrorists at airports had targeted Latinos, blacks, Middle Easterners and others.

Education

61 What is the average educational level of Hispanics?

According to the 2010 Census, about 63 percent of Hispanics over the age of 25 in the United States had completed high school, compared to 87 percent of all adults over 25. For bachelor's degrees in this age group, the comparison was about 14 percent to 30 percent. However, the gap is closing. Census Bureau and Pew data showed that in 2012 the proportion of 18- to 24-year-old Hispanic high school graduates who enrolled in college surpassed that of non-Hispanic whites, 49 percent to 47 percent. Because Hispanic high school graduation rates are lower, though, the proportion of all people in that age group enrolling for college is lower for Hispanics.

62 Do Hispanics come to the United States for schooling?

Education can motivate families to come here, but most Hispanic students in U.S. schools were born here. Hispanic enrollment reached several milestones in 2011 and 2012. College enrollment among Hispanics exceeded 2 million and they became the largest minority group in college, making up 16.5 percent of enrollment. In two-year colleges, they make up more than a quarter of the enrollment. In public elementary schools, Hispanic children comprised

24.7 percent of enrollment. In terms of international students on college campuses, Mexico contributed 2 percent of international students in 2012-2013.

63 Do Hispanic families value education?

A 2010 AP/Univision poll found that 87 percent of Hispanics rated higher education as either important or extremely important, while 78 percent of the overall U.S. population rated it that way. This was similar to a Pew finding from the year before. However, college graduation rates lag for Hispanics. This has been attributed, in part, to income disparity and reluctance to take on debt or burden families with college costs.

64 Why do so many U.S. schools offer bilingual education?

Defined broadly, bilingual education can be any classroom use of two languages. In the context of immigrants, though, it means classroom approaches that use the native languages of English-language learners. The type of bilingual education used should be based on student needs. Some schools face the challenge of teaching students who speak many different languages. The quality and nature of this kind of bilingual education varies widely.

65 Do Hispanics get special consideration when applying to colleges?

While most colleges have eliminated Affirmative Action programs, some schools still consider race and ethnicity in admission decisions, while others do not. The degree to which it makes a difference across the country is not clear.

66 Are there particular colleges or universities that are more welcoming to Hispanics?

The Hispanic Association of Colleges and Universities lists about 250 member institutions that it says are "Hispanic-serving." That means that the equivalent of 25 percent of the university's full-time undergraduate enrollment is Hispanic. Also, Hispanic Business magazine publishes top 10 lists of schools that it finds are the best graduate schools in business, law, engineering and medicine for Hispanics.

Work & Money

67 What is the median annual personal earnings of Latinos in the United States?

Based on data collected for the Census Bureau's 2011 American Community Survey, the annual personal earnings for U.S.-born Latinos 16 and older who had earnings was $22,400 per year. The figure for foreign-born Latinos was $20,000. The median for the age group regardless of ethnicity was $29,000. These are averages only. There is tremendous range within each classification.

68 What percentage of Latinos live beneath the poverty line?

According to the U.S. Census Bureau, 26.7 percent of Latinos were beneath the poverty line in 2011. This compared to 10 percent for whites, 12.1 percent for Asians and 25.4 percent for blacks.

69 Where are Latinos employed?

According to a 2011 Pew analysis of the Census Bureau's American Community Survey, Latino employment was dispersed. The largest sectors were office and administrative support; installation, repair and production; sales; cleaning; construction; food preparation, and transportation. Each of those seven sectors had between 8.1 percent and 12.3

percent of the Latino workforce. Management jobs were held by 4.8 percent of Latinos and 3.5 percent were in education, training and library jobs. Compared to other Americans, Hispanics were more likely to say that their standard of living is higher than that of their parents and that their children's will be even better.

70 Why do American employers hire people from Latin America to work in agriculture?

It's not just in agriculture. According to Pew, about 742,000 Latinos hold manual labor jobs in the farming, fishing or forestry industries. Data collected from the Urban Institute in 2004 indicated that 15 percent of authorized immigrants and 32 percent of unauthorized immigrants had less than a ninth grade education, making them ineligible for jobs that require at least a high school diploma or General Equivalency Degree. Latinos who are either unauthorized to work in the United States or who have a lower level of education find themselves able to get only low-paid, unregulated jobs doing manual labor.

71 Do Latinos go into business for themselves?

According to a 2013 Geoscape report, the number of Hispanic businesses grew an estimated 40 percent from 2007 to 2013. Additionally, the share of new entrepreneurs who were Latino grew from 10.5 percent in 1996 to 19.5 percent in 2012.

72 Do Latinos compete with Americans for jobs?

Most Latinos are Americans, too. Companies, states and the federal government have a long history of hiring workers from other states or countries during labor shortages or to do jobs that are difficult or low paying. Federal work visa programs are designed specifically to bring in foreign workers for positions that employers have trouble filling from the U.S. labor pool.

73 How many Latinos are in the United States without documentation?

An estimated 8 million out of 11.2 million immigrants are working without documentation in the United States, according to research Pew conducted in 2011.

74 How large is the Latino market in the United States?

At 53 million people and growing, the Latino market has a lot of spending power. In a 2013 report, Nielsen estimated that Latino buying power was $1 trillion in 2010 and would grow to $1.5 trillion in 2015.

75 What percentage of women work outside the home in Latino families?

The proportion of Latinas in the workforce is increasing. According to Pew Research, the labor force participation rate of Latinas is 59 percent, similar to the participation rate for non-Latinas.

Families

76 Are Hispanic families large?

In the 2010 Census, Hispanic families were more likely than other families to have five or more members. The families were also more likely to consist of more than two generations under one roof. Although Hispanic families are the fastest growing part of the population, the birth rate is declining. Also, according to the Census Bureau, Hispanic families were less likely than non-Hispanic white or Asian families to be headed by two parents.

77 How are Hispanic families structured?

It depends. In some, the father may be the head of the household. In others, there might be no father, or the grandmother might have the last word. Families and family norms are shifting. In many cases, members of the extended family can play important roles as grandparents, parents and children may live in the same household.

78 How are elders regarded in Hispanic families?

Hispanic people traditionally are taught to respect those older than themselves and to look to elders for guidance and advice. Rank is important and elders must always be treated with respect. Even if generations live separately, they might live near each other and visit frequently. This varies according to family structure, assimilation and personal choice.

79 At what age do Hispanics marry?

Hispanics get married younger, start having children sooner and have more children than the general U.S. population. This is driven by the immigrant generation and is not as pronounced in successive generations. Pew reports that 15 percent of Hispanic women aged 16 to 25 are married and that this is higher among immigrants. The same holds true with childbirth. Twenty-six percent of 18- and 19-year-old foreign-born Hispanic women have children, compared with 16 percent of same-age second-generation Hispanic women. For the third generation, the rate rose back up to 21 percent.

80 Is it acceptable to date outside of one's culture?

In a 2011 Pew national survey of Hispanics, 87 percent said they would be comfortable if they had a child who married someone who was not Hispanic. The same number said so for a person who was Hispanic but who did not share the same heritage. When it came to religious differences, however, 63 percent said they would be comfortable. Pew reports that 26 percent of Hispanic newlyweds in 2010 married people of other ethnic groups.

Health

81 What are top health concerns for Latinos?

The top causes of death for Latinos are obesity, cardiovascular disease and diabetes, according to the Centers for Disease Control and Prevention. Conditions that disproportionately affect Latinos or some sub-groups are diabetes, asthma, obesity, teen pregnancy, smoking and infant mortality.

82 To what extent do Latinos have health insurance?

According to the Centers for Disease Control and Prevention, about 31.1 percent of Latinos under the age of 65 do not have health insurance. According to Pew research in 2009, 60 percent of Latino adults, whether documented or not, did not have health insurance. Fifteen percent of all Latino adults said that they use private doctors.

83 What issues do Latinos encounter in getting medical care?

Language barriers can be big and can hurt patients. Patients do better when there is a cultural match between them and their health-care professionals. The proportion of Latino doctors is not keeping pace with the Latino population. The Association of American Medical Colleges reported in 2011 that fewer than 8 percent of the nation's medical school applicants in 2011 were Latino. That is less than half the proportion of Latinos in the U.S. population.

84 Are there other issues in getting health care?

Latinos are twice as likely as non-Hispanic blacks and three times as likely as non-Hispanic whites to lack a regular health-care provider, according to the Centers for Disease Control and Prevention. More than 80 percent report receiving health information from alternative sources, such as television and radio.

85 What is the "Hispanic paradox"?

The Hispanic paradox refers to studies showing that although Hispanic communities in the United States tend to have a higher risk factor for illnesses, they tend to have a longer life expectancy than non-Hispanics with the same health problems. Several studies have attributed this to family cohesion.

Culture

86 Do Hispanics have preferences in news outlets?

That depends largely on the language match. Those who are English dominant lean toward English-language TV outlets. Those who prefer Spanish lean toward Spanish-language networks like Univision and Telemundo. According to a 2013 Pew report, this has been shifting toward English. In 2012, 82 percent of Hispanic adults consumed news in English, up from 78 percent in 2006. In that same period, those who consumed news in Spanish dropped from 78 percent to 68 percent, indicating some used media in both languages. The actual use of Spanish also depends on the availability of outlets in that language.

87 How much do Hispanics use the Internet?

Internet use by Hispanics is high and rising, but there is a digital divide among them. According to Pew, Hispanics are more likely to use the Internet if they are U.S.-born, English-dominant, wealthier, more educated or younger. Seventy-eight percent said in 2012 that they used the Internet to send or receive email. This was up 14 percentage points from 2009. Seventy-six percent of Hispanic Internet users said they access the Internet on a cellphone and 28 percent said they used social networking sites such as Twitter.

88 How do entertainment media portray Hispanics?

According to a report commissioned by the National Hispanic Media Coalition about popular media, "non-Latinos report seeing Latinos in stereotypically negative or subordinate roles (gardeners, maids, dropouts, and criminals) most often in television and film. People exposed to negative entertainment or news narratives about Latinos and/or immigrants hold the most unfavorable and hostile views about both groups."

89 What is a telenovela?

A telenovela is a "limited-run" television drama that is very popular in Latin America and has had success in the United States and elsewhere. Telenovelas share similarities but have distinctive qualities from U.S. traditional soap operas. The run time for telenovelas are a fixed duration, with episodes shown five to six days a week and an average of 120 episodes per telenovela. According to Pew, much of Univision's success has been from entertainment programming such as the telenovela "Amores Verdaderos."

90 What is the significance of luminarias on Christmas Eve?

During "Navidad Hispana" it is common to find luminarias, lit with candles or by electricity, at the homes of Hispanic families and families all around the world. The luminarias are lit in remembrance of giving light to Mary and Joseph as they searched for lodging to give birth to Jesus. Today, luminarias are part of more secular celebrations. There are large displays in the state of New Mexico.

91 What is the Day of Three Kings?

This is a Christian holiday celebrated on Jan. 6. It is referred to as Dia De Los Reyes in many Spanish-speaking countries. The holiday celebrates the biblical visitation of the Magi to the birth of Jesus.

92 What is Cinco de Mayo?

Cinco de Mayo, which means May 5, is a Mexican holiday recalling victory over France in the 1862 Battle of Puebla, which occurred during the Franco-Mexican War. Cinco de Mayo festivities include parades, street festivals, mariachi music and special foods in both Mexico and the United States. In the United States, Cinco de Mayo is considered a celebration of Mexican culture. Cinco de Mayo is not equivalent to the Fourth of July. Mexico celebrates its independence from Spain on Sept. 16. Hispanics of other nationalities celebrate different holidays related to their own countries' traditions.

93 What is the Day of the Dead?

The Day of the Dead, a combination of Catholic and indigenous spiritual traditions, is celebrated mostly in central Mexico and has gained some popularity in the United States. Friends and family gather to honor and celebrate those who have passed. The music, food, decorations and festivities take place on Nov. 2, "Dia de Los Muertos." Graves are covered with flowers and gifts for the deceased. Nov. 1 is All Saints Day. People of several Christian faiths celebrate these holidays.

94 What is a quinceañera?

A quinceañera is a Hispanic celebration of a girl's 15th birthday, signifying her transition from youth to adulthood. This is both a social and religious event and, like many other Hispanic traditions, emphasizes the importance of family. A quinceañera typically begins with a mass that is attended by the girl's parents, grandparents, godparents and family. The mass is followed by a reception with food, family, music, dancing and more. In past times, the quinceañera signified that a girl was prepared for marriage. In contemporary times, it tends to mean that a girl is ready to begin formal dating. Some families will throw a quinceañero for a son.

Food

95 I know about tortillas and tacos and rice and beans. Are there other kinds of Latino foods?

Mexican food is frequently generalized in the United States to represent all Hispanic and Latin American foods, but it does not. People might assume that all Latinos eat Mexican foods such as tacos but they are not characteristic of very many countries. Caribbean and coastal country cuisine consists of fish and seafood while other Latin American countries such as Argentina, a major producer of meat, are known for meat dishes. Latino cuisine is heavily influenced by foods and spices indigenous to the hemisphere such as peppers, chiles and corn-based products as well as African and European ingredients. Maize (corn) based products include tortillas, tamales and Salvadoran pupusas. Not all Latinos like the foods of their ancestral countries. Some have never eaten them.

96 What are differences among Latin American and Hispanic cuisines?

There are several. A large factor is the roots of the countries. Cuban cuisine has Spanish, African and Caribbean influences. Argentinian cuisine is a blend of indigenous, Spanish and Italian cooking. Brazilian cuisine has African and European roots. Cuisines can also vary from region to region within a country, depending on the availability of ingredients or local tastes.

97 Is Latino food healthy?

That depends on how it is prepared. Dishes can be prepared to be healthier than how they're traditionally prepared, such as baking churros instead of frying them. Additionally, salsas, refried beans and dishes such as quesadillas, enchiladas and huevos rancheros can be prepared with fruits and vegetables.

98 What is Tex-Mex food?

Tex-Mex food combines Texan and Mexican cuisines. It is considered by some to be a regional American cuisine rather than an authentic Mexican cuisine. You might also try New Mexican or Cal-Mex food.

99 What is salsa?

Salsa is Spanish for sauce. There are several types of sauces, and different countries have local styles of it. Mexican-style tomato-based salsa has become popular in the United States. Since at least 1992, there have been reports that salsa has surpassed ketchup as America's favorite condiment. This is hard to judge, as sales can be measured by quantity sold, value or frequency of use. Salsa also refers to a Caribbean dance style popularized in New York City with Cuban and Puerto Rican influences.

100 Are Latino foods spicy?

Some are and some are not. Some Latino foods get their spiciness from peppers. The heat, as measured on the Scoville scale, varies. A jalepeño is in the 3,500-8,000 range on the Scoville scale while varieties of the habanero pepper sit in the 350,000-855,000 range. That's hot.

Resources

Books

Gonzales, Manuel G. Mexicanos: *A History of Mexicans in the United States*. 2nd ed. Bloomington: Indiana University Press, 2009.

Gonzalez, Juan. *Harvest of Empire: A History of Latinos in America*. Revised. New York: Penguin Books, 2011.

Mintz, Steven, ed. *Mexican American Voices: A Documentary Reader*. 2nd ed. Malden: Wiley-Blackwell, 2009.

Novas, Himilce. *Everything You Need to Know About Latino History*. Revised. New York: Plume, 2008.

Rodriguez, Clara E. *Changing Race: Latinos, The Census and the History of Ethnicity in the United States*. New York: NYU Press, 2000.

Skidmore, Thomas E., Peter H. Smith and James N. Green. *Modern Latin America*. 7th ed. Oxford University Press, 2009.

Stafford, Jim. *Puerto Ricans' History and Promise: Americans Who Cannot Vote*. Philadelphia: Mason Crest Publishers, 2006.

Suarez, Ray. *Latino Americans: The 500-Year Legacy That Shaped a Nation*. New York: Celebra Trade, 2013.

Tutino, John, ed. *Mexico and Mexicans in the Making of the United States*. Austin: University of Texas Press, 2012.

Encyclopedias

Herrera-Sobek, María, ed. *Celebrating Latino Folklore: An Encyclopedia of Cultural traditions*. Santa Barbara: ABC-CLIO, 2012.

Oboler, Suzanne, and Deena J. González, eds. *The Oxford Encyclopedia of Latinos and Latinas in the United States.* Oxford: Oxford University Press, 2005.

Videos

National Latino Communications Center, and NLCC Educational Media. *1. Quest for a Homeland. 2. Struggle in the Fields.* National Latino Communications Center. Distributed by NLCC Educational Media, 1996.

---. *Taking Back the Schools. Fighting for Political Power.* National Latino Communications Center: Distributed by NLCC Educational Media, 1996.

Onyx Films et al. *Harvest of Empire: The Untold Story of Latinos in America.* Onyx Films; EVS Communications, 2012.

Fritz, Sonia. *Latino Americans.* Washington, D.C.: PBS Distribution, 2013.

Chicano! History of the Mexican American Civil Rights Movement. Video. NLCC Educational Media, 1996.

The Graduates/Los Graduados. http://itvs.org/films/graduates. ITVS, 2013.

20th Century with Mike Wallace: *Hispanics in America.* PBS. 2009.

Websites

American GI Forum: http://www.agifusa.org/

Center for Immigration Studies: http://cis.org/

League of United Latin American Citizens: https://lulac.org/

Mexican American Legal Defense and Educational Fund: http://www.maldef.org

Movimiento Estudiantil Chicano de Aztlán: http://www.nationalmecha.org/about.html

National Association of Hispanic Journalists: www.nahj.org/

National Public Radio: http://www.npr.org/blogs/
codeswitch/2014/01/21/263502571/a-new-poll-takes-a-look-
at-views-from-latino-america
Pew Hispanic Center: www.pewhispanic.org/
Urban Institute: http://www.urban.org/

Also in This Series

- 100 Questions and Answers About Indian Americans
- 100 Questions and Answers About Americans
- 100 Questions and Answers About Arab Americans
- 100 Questions and Answers About East Asian Cultures
- 100 Questions, 500 Nations: A Guide to Native America

For Copies

Copies of this guide in paperback or ebook formats may be ordered from Amazon.

For a volume discount on copies or a special edition customized and branded for your university or organization, contact David Crumm Media, LLC at info@DavidCrummMedia.com.

For more information and further discussion visit: news.jrn.msu.edu/culturalcompetence

If you enjoyed this book, you may also enjoy

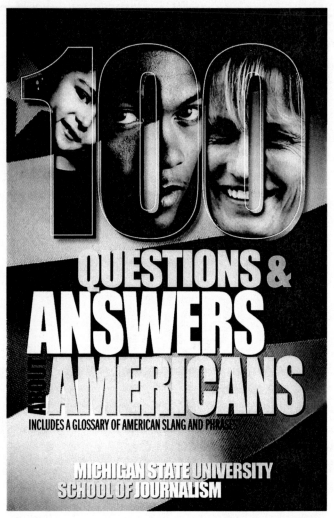

This questions and answers guide from the Michigan
State University School of Journalism provides 100
answers to basic questions about Americans.

http://news.jrn.msu.edu/culturalcompetence/

ISBN: 978-1-939880-20-8

If you enjoyed this book, you may also enjoy

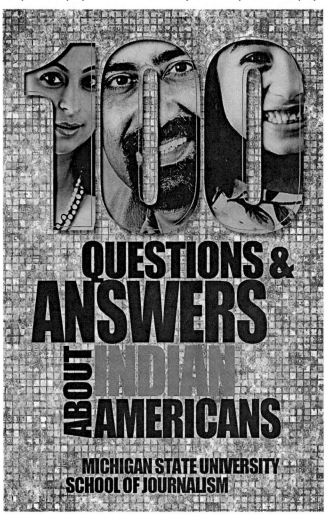

This questions and answers guide from the Michigan
State University School of Journalism provides 100
answers to basic questions about Indian Americans.

http://news.jrn.msu.edu/culturalcompetence/

ISBN: 978-1-939880-00-0

If you enjoyed this book, you may also enjoy

This questions and answers guide from the Michigan State University School of Journalism provides 100 answers to basic questions about East Asian cultures.

http://news.jrn.msu.edu/culturalcompetence/

ISBN: 978-939880-50-5

If you enjoyed this book, you may also enjoy

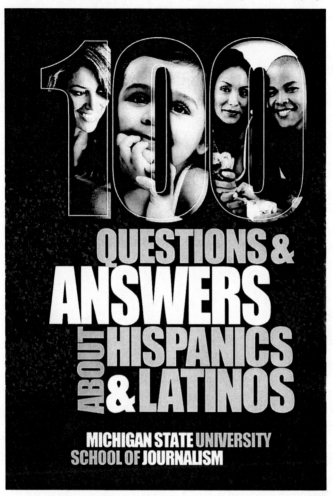

This questions and answers guide from the Michigan State University School of Journalism provides 100 answers to basic questions about Hispanics and Latinos.

http://news.jrn.msu.edu/culturalcompetence/

ISBN: 978-1-939880-44-4